D0868529

WRECKiNG JOURNAL

PaRT 2

Reviews are the soul of every publishing author. Please take a minute to leave us a review. Just scan the QR code, it will take you to our Author Page.

Follow us:

Art and design by Color Doe Smile

© 2021 by Color Doe Smile. All rights reserved

This book or any portion thereof may not be reproduced or used in any manner whatsoever without the express written permission of the publisher except for the use of brief quotations in a book review.

support@colordoesmile.com

Some of the activities you will find in this book may not be appropriate for children without supervision.

PROFILE INFO

ADD A RECENT
PHOTO OF YOU

WHAT'S YOUR NAME?

WRITE YOUR NAME BACKWARDS

WHICH 3 WORDS DESCRIBE YOU?

------------------------   ------------------------   ------------------------

WHAT WOULD YOUR ROCK STAR NAME BE?

NAME 3 PERSONS WITH WHOM YOU WILL SHARE THE JOURNAL

------------------------   ------------------------   ------------------------

GIVE AN AUTOGRAPH

We are back with the new edition of Wrecking Journal. For all of you that have finished the first edition, it's now the time for some new challenges. You will see that this new journal respects the same theme so you will enjoy it at least the same as the first one.

If this is your first Wrecking Journal then you should know that there is no right way of going through the journals. To finish this one and then you can start the first one. That's the beauty of wrecking: there is no order in the wrecking process.

- Wrecking is not about destroying -
- Wrecking it's about CREATING -

It's about unleashing your creativity without borders. It's about expressing yourself and showing your uniqueness.

That's why this book will be unique because so are YOU. Everything is unique about you and that will be seen in every wrecking creation of this book.

Expressing yourself is the best way to know yourself. So get creative and start

WRECKING

DON'T LET THIS PAGE EMPTY

DEAR ARTIST,

THIS JOURNAL WAS MADE TO BE USED NO MATTER WHERE YOU FIND YOURSELF. JUST KEEP IN MIND TO HAVE AS MUCH FUN AS YOU CAN WHILE COMPLETING THE TASKS. IT'S TIME TO START AN ADVENTURE. SO STOP READING AND START

WRECKING!!!

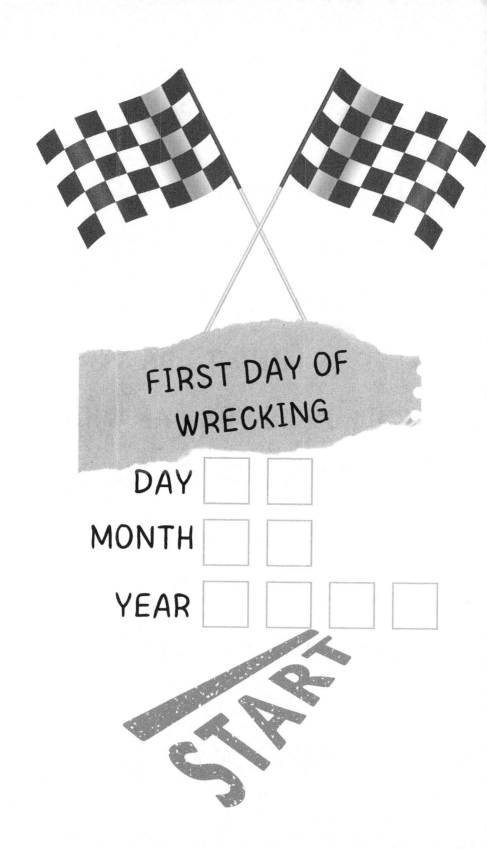

SUGGESTIONS

There isn't a good way or a bad way to complete the tasks.

Let your imagination run wild and don't limit yourself.

Complete the tasks at your own choice and desired time.

Every task it's open to interpretation. Only you decide how to complete it.

Most importantly:
Have Fun!!!

Lots and Lots of Fun!!!

DON'T LET THIS PAGE EMPTY

"Creativity is more than just being DIFFERENT... Making the simple AWESOMELY SIMPLE, that's CREATIVITY. "

CHARLES MINGUS

NAMASTE

PRIVET

HELLO

Say hello in different ways and in different languages.
You can draw, write, glue or anything you have in mind.

NǏ HǍO

BUNĂ

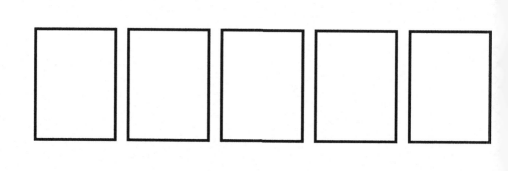

FINGERPRINT PAGE
Fill the pages with fingerprints.

"Z" LETTER PAGE

Fill the pages with the letter Z. It's up to you what you add.

WEL

COME

Find a way to keep the journal wide open so that it could be used as an ENTRANCE MAT. Use it for at least one day at your home entrance.

FOREST
Create a forest starting from this tree.

Find a way to create ice cream on this page.

This is going to be a bit messy...

FAVORITE PIZZA'S

Now this is quite a tricky challenge. Next time you eat pizza place a slice on this page, close the journal and press. Will it have the shape of a pizza printed on the left page?

Draw it, sketch it, stick it, glue it. Just place it on the "sky".

AIRPLANES

ROAD TRIP

Where would you go?

MASON JARS

Fill the jars with you like and label them.

CREATIVE WRECKING METHOD OF YOUR OWN

Date ------------

MASKS PAGE

Tear this page and use it to create your own mask
Carnival, superhero, protection mask. You choose!

RAIN

Describe. draw, or paint a rainy day.

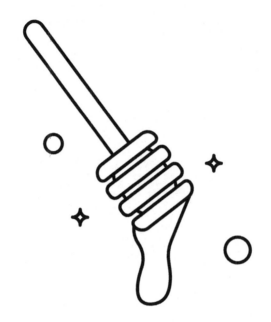

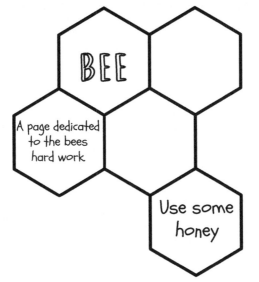

BEE

A page dedicated to the bees hard work

Use some honey

BUILD YOUR CITY

Using the lines on the pages create a city from scratch.

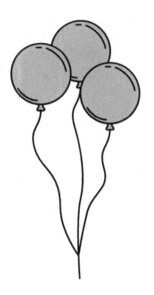

BALOONS
FESTIVAL

Raise as many
balloons as possible
and as many types as
possible.

SEAL YOUR SECRETS

On the next 2 pages write some secrets or sensitive information and then find a way to seal the secret. Sew or glue the pages.

CLASSIFIED CLASSIFIED CLASSIFIED CLASSIFIED CLASSIFIED CLASSIFIED

TOP SECRET

FARM LIFE

How would life at the farm look for you?

ROCKY PAGE

Fill the page with small stones, close it and
jump up and down on the journal.

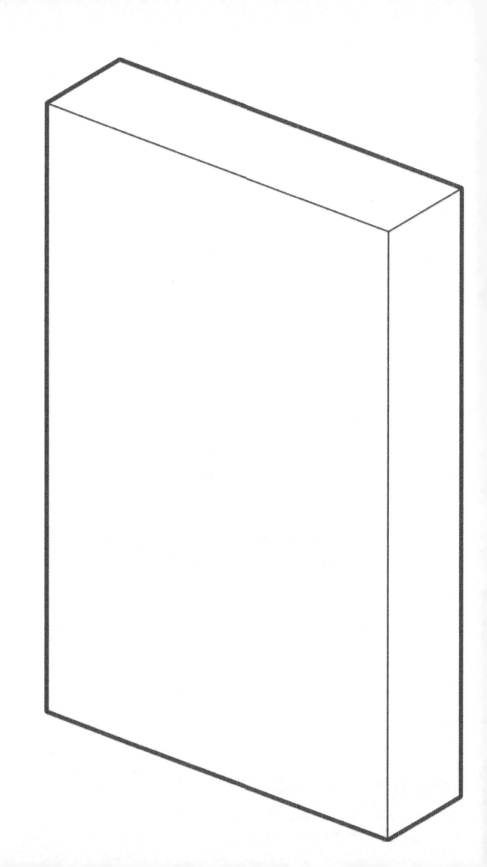

CEREAL BOX

Redesign the box of your favorite cereals.

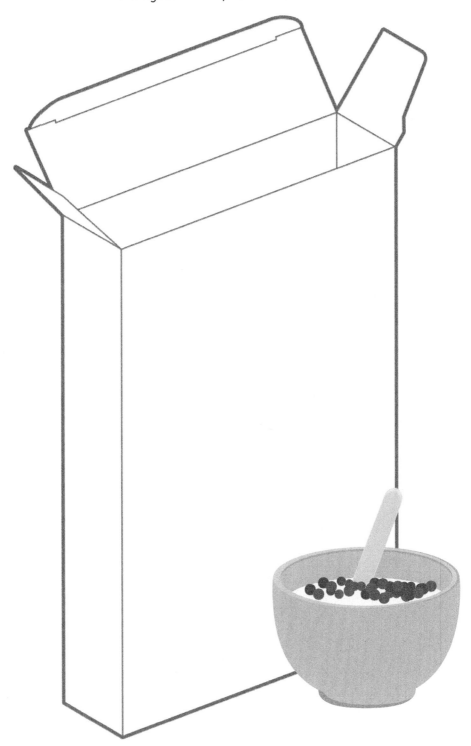

YOUR HOME

Starting from the left page
recreate the exterior or
interior of your home or the
one of your ideal home.

MUSIC PAGE

Dedicate this page to music and to what this represents for you.

ORIGAMI UMBRELLA

Cut this page ad create from it an origami umbrella and then add it to page on the left. You can also add other umbrellas there.

SWAP PAGE

Swap this page with a page from a magazine, a book or even a newspaper.
Find a clever way to attach the new page in here.

No need to stop at only 1 page!

PICNIC DAY
Starting from the picnic basket create
an amazing picnic day

HOLIDAY POSTCARDS

Design your own postcards that you
would like to send to the ones you love.

CREATIVE WRECKING METHOD OF YOUR OWN

~~~~~~

~~~~~~

Date ~~~~~~~~~~~~

CATS

DOG

Fill the pages with cats and
dogs. You can dedicate one
page for each animal or
combine them.

HALLOWEEN THEME

Create the perfect Halloween night, with
costumes, decorations, and candy.

FINISH

BOARD GAME

Create your own board game. Make
your rules, your narrative, your theme.

START

EGG RECONSTRUCTION

Glue eggshell on the shape to create a large egg.

COLLECTOR

WRAPPING

Gather here the wrapping from all the candy's that you will eat from now on.

HOUSE TREE

We provide you with ladders for 2 houses. It's
your turn to create the houses and the trees.

SPACE MISSION

Draw your own rocket launch and
the place you'd like to go.

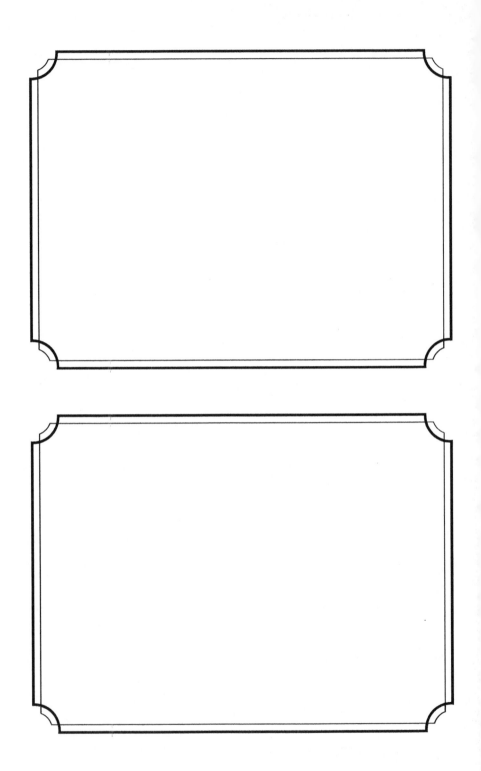

ALL SEASONS

Capture all seasons and if possible in the same landscape.

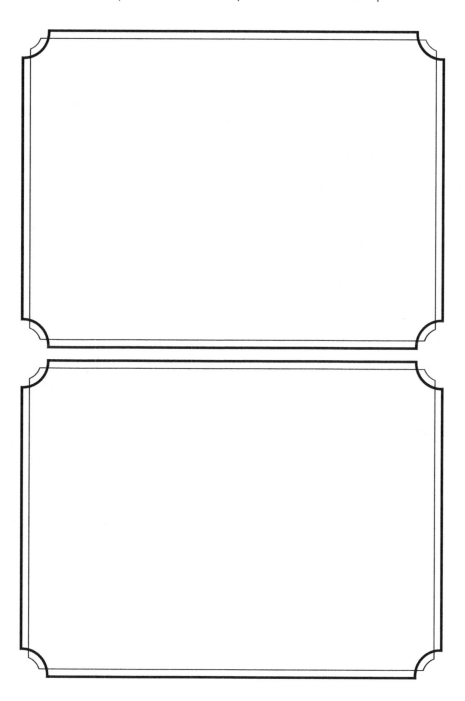

BORROWED PAGE

Borrow the page on the right to a
friend, or a family member. It's their
choice what they do with the page.
Just let them know to return it and
then attach it back to the journal.

BIGGEST 3 WISHES

You have a genie that can fulfill 3
wishes. Which are those wishes?

YOUR BIRTHDAY

Add cake, people, gifts and
what would you like to have
at your birthday party!

CREATIVE WRECKING METHOD OF YOUR OWN

Date ------------------

ONE COLOR PAGE

On this page, you can use only one color of
your choice. Use different nuances and also
you can glue cut-off pieces.

WASHING MACHINE CHALLENGE

Fill this page front & back with what you
want, text, drawing, painting and then fold it
and place it in a pocket of one of your
clothes that need to we washed. After it's
washed, dry it and glue attach it back to
the journal.

BEACH
DAY

Gather on these pages all the things that
would represent a perfect beach day.

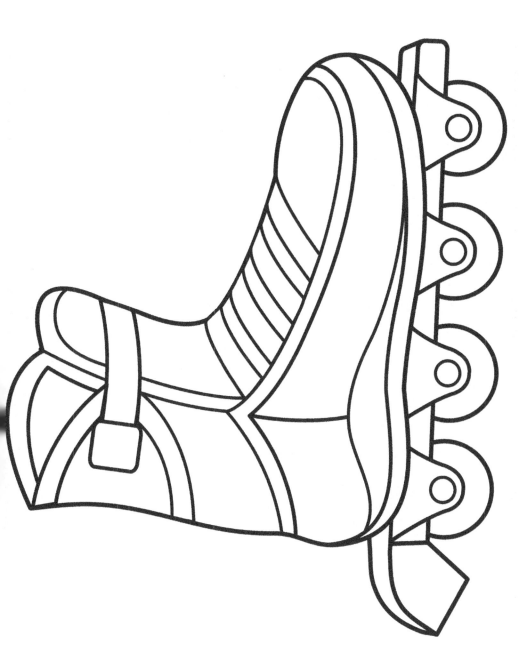

ROLLER SKATES DESIGN
Create your own design for roller skates. Make them look different.

SPORTS PAGE

DAILY NEWS

REAL FOREST

Gather all sorts of leaves and cover both pages from top to bottom.

STORY CREATION

Cut words from the right page and create a story here.
You choose the subject. No need to use all the words.
Also, add other words by writing or gluing.

LARGESTODDPLAYGROUNDBLESSINGPHANTOM
PROTECTFORGIVENCOMMERCIALJUICEJUNIORRED
DOZENBONUSAMATEURCAGECREATORACTUALITY
AGAINBELLYFULBITERCRAZYCREATIONMAGICGRIP
DISTINCTPOETRYEDGEFLAVORINGPRAYERGIVING
FEETMOUNTAINRECORDBAMBOOTRUSTCAPTURED
ABOVEEIGHTSANITARYBALCONYLIMITLESSTIN
HAPPYDESCRIPTIONFIASCOORANGEGOLDFISH
FOCUSSKYPORTRAITINDUSTRYKINGHOMESICK
MOUNTAINACTIONPLAYTIMEPEPPERMINT
BELIEVABLEFEELINGFRENCHBECOMEPAPERSTAR
TACTICGIVINGPIECECHAPTERPOWERLONELYLADY
BIRDJEWELARRIVALBORDERMIXERAGENTHORSE
LONERMINIMALLANDSCAPEFASTRISKYNEARFATE
EVERLASTINGBENEATHFOAMVIRTUALSIXRANCH
HORIZONSEARCHCHEFFIASCOBADBEESWAXCANVAS
BABOONHOLDUPDOPEISLANDBAKECROPBUMPCHERR
YINNOCENTBASKETLARGEPASSION
I I I I I I YOU YOU YOU WE WE WE ME ME ME
THEM THEM THEY WITH WITH WITH CAN CAN CAN DO
DO DO DO DO WHEN WHEN WHEN THEN THEN THIS
THIS THIS THAT THAT THAT THESE THESE THESE
WILL WILL WILL DON'T DON'T DON'T CAN'T CAN'T

FAVORITE DESSERTS

Find a way to show your favorite 4 desserts.

INSECTARIUM

Gather a collection of insects, real or not.

CRYSTAL BALL

What can you see inside the crystal ball?
Use one for the future on one for the past.

CREATIVE WRECKING METHOD OF YOUR OWN

Date --------

BURNING PAGE

Tear the page out of the
book, then burn it in a way
it takes a shape. Add it on
the left page.

 WARNING: This activity requires adult supervision.

GOOD THOUGHTS

Tear each quote and then pass it on to someone that needs to
be encouraged. Let's make the world a better place.

Never Stop Dreaming!

You're Beautiful.

Small Steps Every Day.

Be you! Do You! For You!

Keep Going!

Smile! It's Free!

Enjoy your own company.

Do It Now!
Sometimes "Later"
becomes "Never"

You Are Enough.

A FRIEND FROM OUT OF SPACE

How do you think it looks like?

HAPPY VS ANGRY

Happy vs Angry Girl

TREASURE MAP

Create a treasure map
starting from the letter X.

EARTHY COLORS

Paint both pages with what colors you like, keep the color thick
Then drag the journal on the sidewalk, grass, mud, or any outside
surfaces. while keeping the journal open on these two pages. TIP:
Drag the journal before the paint dries.

SOMEONE ELSE'S WRECKING

Give the journal or just this page to someone else
so he can wreck it his own way. No restrictions!

MAGAZINES FACE
Use all sorts of magazines, newspaper or other materials to
create two different characters.

STRING IT

Get creative with string threads.

OLD WARDROBE
COLLECTION
Use pieces cut out from old clothes you're not wearing anymore and gather them here in harmony.

SAILING

Create a paper boat using this page. Give it a try on water to see how it floats and after that find a way to anchor it back in the journal.

SCHOOL
AUTOGRAPHS

Take the journal at school and let all
your friends and colleagues sign it.

PAPER BRACELET

Come up with an idea of how to create paper bracelets from these pages. Create something fashionable.

MAGAZINE COVER

Use parts from different magazines to create the cover of YOUR magazine.

CREATIVE WRECKING METHOD OF YOUR OWN

‒‒‒

‒‒‒

Date ‒‒‒‒‒‒‒‒‒‒‒‒

ADJÖ

LA REVEDERE

GOODBYE

Say goodbye in different ways and in different languages
You can draw, write, glue or anything you have in mind.

GÖRÜŞÜRÜZ!

ZÀI JIÀN

Congratulations

WRECKING JOURNAL PART II

COMPLETED

FINISH

LAST DAY OF WRECKING

DAY ☐ ☐

MONTH ☐ ☐

YEAR ☐ ☐ ☐ ☐

Reviews are the soul of every publishing author. Please take a minute to leave us a review. Just scan the QR code, it will take you to our Author Page.

Follow us:

Art and design by Color Doe Smile

© 2021 by Color Doe Smile. All rights reserved

This book or any portion thereof may not be reproduced or used in any manner whatsoever without the express written permission of the publisher except for the use of brief quotations in a book review.

support@colordoesmile.com

Some of the activities you will find in this book may not be appropriate for children without supervision.